THE PREOCCUPATIONS OF `ABI

BUKHARAN NONCONFORMIST

(An Analysis and List of His Writings)

EDWARD A. ALLWORTH

Contents

Tables and Illustrations

Preface

During the 1920s and 1930s, The New York Public Library (NYPL) and the Library of Congress (LC) of the U.S.A. acquired for their collections at least 10 books and pamphlets written by the subject of this analysis, `Abdalrauf Abdurahim-oghli Fitrat (1886-1938) and published between 1923 and 1927, inclusively. (see Nationalities of the Soviet East. Publications and Writing Systems (1971). Long held in uncatalogued files, nevertheless, these publications and hundreds of others from those years in the local languages remained accessible to students, emigrants and scholars. The NYPL made works available beginning from the decades of their acquisition – a time contemporaneous with Professor Fitrat's most productive period. Fortunately for scholarship, this occurred before Central Asia's Communist Party ideologists in Tashkent all but silenced Professor Fitrat and his colleagues and then brought about his execution and that of others as "enemies of the people."

The NYPL in 1996, at the initiative of the Chief of its Slavic and Baltic Division, Dr. Edward Kasinec, moved to preserve these valuable and very fragile rare books and to produce a temporary paper catalogue compiled for users by Nermin Eren.

In 1999, under grants from The New York State Library, Conservation/Preservation Program, Albany, New York, and from the Center for Research Libraries, Slavic and East European Microfilming Project, Chicago, Illinois, a newer undertaking to bring these materials under bibliographic control has been managed by Robert H. Davis, Jr., a librarian in the NYPL's

Slavic and Baltic Division. It has proceeded with the compilation of cataloging information especially in order to insert records of the Central Asian and related publications from the
1920s and 1930s into the major U.S. bibliographic utilities,
OCLC and RLIN. This step meant to make the presence of these
materials known via its online catalogue for the benefit of
scholars and students worldwide. Users may reach the appropriate catalogue for bibliographic citations (cataloging records)
through the Internet via NYPL's public access catalog CATNYP
by dialing URL http:\\catnyp.nypl.org

The author of the present analysis, the compiler of the at-
tached list of writings, especially thanks Shaahmad Mutalaw,
Dr. Diloram Nishanov and family, Munevver Olgun, Dr. Shahr-
banou Tadjbakhsh and Ibrahim Yuksel for making important
contributions to enrichment of this list of `Abdalrauf Fitrat's
many writings and publications.

The compiler of this Bibliography also especially acknowl-
edges the good advice given earlier by Professor William L.
Hanaway regarding certain Tajik entries. Generous counsel and
friendly guidance of citizens of Türkiye and emigrants from
Bukhara, from Crimea, Kazan, Turkistan and from Ufa, in the
earliest stages of this research several decades ago, in Türkiye
and Germany, greatly educated the author of this article about
`Abdalrauf Fitrat and his writings. Some of those good people
include Dr. Halûk Avanoglu, Dr. Saadat Ishaqiy Chaghatay, Dr.
Tahir Chaghatay, Mlle. Gaspirali, Mr. Veli Kayyum-Khan,

Professor Ahmad Jan Ibrahim Okay, Dr. A. Oktay and Mme. Saida Hanim Oktay, Mr. Ahmad Naim Nusratullahbek (Oktem), Mr. Nadir Ricaloglu, and Professor Ahmet Zeki Velidi (Togan). Professor Robert Austerlitz, Dr. Baymirza Hayit, Professor Timur Kocaoglu, Professor Hisao Komatsu, Mr. Ibrahim Pourhadi, and others, at different times and in various collections, graciously helped the compiler locate some of the important, scarce writings listed in the Bibliography, below.

In the following essay, numbers inserted after textual citations of specific works refer to the sequence recorded in the Bibliography of `Abdalrauf Fitrat's writings.

I.   THE PREOCCUPATIONS OF `ABDALRAUF FITRAT, BUKHARAN NONCONFORMIST

A.   The Preparation

The scant historical record reveals little out of the ordinary that might have disaffected `Abdalrauf Abdurahim-oghli (H.1304/ A.D.1886-1938), during his young years in a middle-class Central Asian family. Starting in the last decade and a half of the nineteenth century, he grew up as a native-speaker in Tajik-speaking Bukhara. He lost touch with one parent in early childhood. His father, Abdurahimbay, a devout Muslim and literate, widely-traveled merchant, left the city and the family for Marghilan and ultimately, Qashqar, in East Turkistan.

The boy's mother, Mustaf Bibi, called affectionately Bibijan, saw him through the standard Muslim primary school (maktab) curriculum of the region. He enrolled for further training in one of Bukhara's 200 religious seminaries – the Mir-i Arab madrassah. It stood nearly at the top of the list of upper seminaries at that time and enjoyed support from one of the largest madrassah endowments.[1] Yet, only a few years later, `Abdalrauf, basing himself upon personal experience, included the Mir-i Arab madrassah in a scathing generalization about the ineffectiveness characterizing all Bukharan seminaries. He must have received his own excellent education mainly at home. Mustaf Bibi, a

---

[1] Abd-ur-Rauf, <u>Razskazy indiiskago puteshestvennika (Bukhara, kak ona est')</u>. Trans. from Persian by A. N. Kondrat'ev. Samarkand: Izdanie Makhmud-Khodzha Begbudi, 1913, pp. 19-22, 24-25.

gentle-natured, highly literate woman, made a poetry and book lover of her son at an early age by reading with him the main poets of Western Asia and the Middle East, especially Bedil, Fuzuliy, Nawaiy, and the like.[2]

In his brief autobiography, composed in 1929, Professor Fitrat relates: "I was born in 1884 (sic) in Bukhara, where I was subject to one of the darkest religious centers and darkest systems of administration [that existed]....After primary school (maktab), I entered a religious seminary (madrassah) and took lessons, said prayers [and] was a fanatic Muslim. In Bukhara, I even opposed the early beginnings of the movement of Reformists (Jadids)."[3]

Consequently, as a pupil, he missed the direct experience of a more modern pedagogy through Muslim Reformist (usul-i jadid) schooling. It had reached Bukhara late, and faltered in the Amirate of Bukhara owing to stern official and conservative religious opposition to allowing those innovative private schools to compete with the parochial system's exclusion from the curriculum of science, arithmetic, geography, and the like,

[2] Hämidullä Baltäbayew, "Namä'lum *Fiträt*," Yashlik no. 4 (1990), p. 34; Sabir Mirwäliew, Ozbek ädibläri (ikhchäm ädäbiy portretlär). Tashkent: Ozbekistan Respublikäsi Fänlär Äkädemiyäsi "FÄN" Näshriyati, 1993, p. 18; Näim Kärimaw, Erik Kärimaw, Sheräli Turdiew, compilers, Chin sewish. She'rlär, drämälär, mäqalälär. Tashkent: Ghäfur Ghulam namidägi Ädäbiyat wä Sän'ät Näshriyati, 1996, pp. 4, 245-46; Sewärä Käramätilläkhojäewä, "Qälbimgä mängu muhrlängän...Äbduräuf Fiträt häqidä khatirälär," Täfäkkur, no. 2 (1996), pp. 67-68.

[3] Fiträt, "Yapishmägän gäjäklär. Ortaq Baybulätawgä achiq khät," Qzil Ozbekistan nos. 15-16 (Sept. 15-16, 1929). Reprinted by Näim Kärimaw, Erik Kärimaw and Sheräli Turdiew, comps., in Chin sewish. Tashkent: Ghäfur Ghulam namidägi Adäbiyat wä Sän'ät Näshriyati, 1996, p. 245.

and its emphasis upon religion, memorization and convention. Though he did not benefit personally from primary schooling under the Reformist methodology, he soon associated with the senior Reformists, and later became their stellar protégé.

As a result of these limitations, an inquiry into what made this extraordinary Central Asian intellectual, social activist and professional academician into the nonconformist that he became from early adulthood onward has to look elsewhere. In documented history, `Abdalrauf Fitrat first appears on the public scene around 1910, at the age of 24, with a mind already formed but an outlook still constrained by the relatively closed life in the capital of the Amirate. For rising generations, he appeared at an opportune moment in the developing educational affairs of the country.

When the leaders of the Reformist movement in Bukhara sought to strengthen their teaching of renewal among the generation of young Central Asians, as well as among the broader population, these Jadids initiated several actions. Above all, they organized and supported the establishment of of New (phonetic) Method (usul-i jadid) schools, published newspapers in the vernacular, encouraged new-style original drama and theater, and, specifically for their pupils, wrote textbooks mainly in the Turki language – publications meant to replace the old, obscure manuscript texts by famous mystic poets. Those writers composed so much of that literature in Persian, works long imposed upon young Central Asian schoolchildren of all languages.

Less well known than those measures taken by Reformists, came another kind of action, one certainly less direct but probably more fundamental in exerting a long-range impact upon people in Central Asia. In March 1909, Bukharan Reformists had founded an organization that they called Partnership for Bukhara the Noble (Shirkat-i Bukhara-yi Sharif). It sent ʿOsman Khoja Polat-oghli (1878-1968), his brother ʿAta Khoja, and Mazhar Makhzum, Burhan Makhzum-oghli, Muqim Bek and Hamidkhoja, to Bakhchesaray or Istanbul to acquaint themselves with schools for studying the phonetic method (usul-i sawtiya) for teaching and learning to read.[4] The sponsors issued guidelines for a non-profit association established in Istanbul by means of which they could implement this program to send Central Asian students to that City. In H.1327/A.D.1909, they called the new, open organization The Bukharan Benevolent Society for the Propagation of the Sciences (Bukhara Taʿamim Maʿarif Jemʿiyyet Khayriyasi). The Statute stipulated as the Society's sole aim the sending of students, ages 10-15 years, from Bukhara and Turkistan to Istanbul and providing stipends for those from poor families unable to cover their expenses.[5]

---

[4] Näzrulla Yoldashew, Äbduräuf Fiträtning "Rähbär-i näjat," ("Qutqäruw yoli") äsäridän mukhtäsär fäsllär. Bukhara: Bukhara Näshriyati, 1996, pp. 3-4.

[5] Bukhara Taʿamim Maʿarif Jemʿiyyet Khayriyasining Nizamname ve Khat-i Hareketidir. Dar-i Saʿdat: Wazirkhan (Metin) Matbaʿasinda Tabʿ Olinmishdir, 1327 (A.D.1909), p. 7.

A year later (H.1328/A.D.Dec. 2, 1910), Bukharan Reformists founded a secret organization, Society for the Education of Children (Jam`iyat-i Tarbiya-yi Atfal) in Bukhara. It adopted the common, general goal of driving ignorance and illiteracy out of the population. Unlike the Bukharan Benevolent Society, the Society for the Education of Children also undertook several social and political tasks: to compete with conservatives, to inform people about the illegal deeds of government officials, to explain to the public that the wealth of the state should not be treated as the Amir's private fortune (and be deposited in Russian banks); and, the Society attempted to educate the public concerning the need to rid the area of religious fanaticism and strife.[6]

The Society for the Education of Children sent 15 students to Istanbul in 1911 and 30 in 1912. A student in one earlier group, `Abdalrauf Abdurahim-oghli Fitrat, received that privilege beginning in spring, 1910, and spent about four productive years in Istanbul, which he had reached via Persia. Sadriddin `Ayniy, Tajik annalist, author and member of Bukharan Reformist circles, wrote in 1920-21: "In Spring, 1910, Fitrat afandi with Muqimiddinbek had traveled via Iran to Istanbul. Fitrat afandi, in reality, was one of the most able of Bukhara's students; he had specialized in the old literature and sciences of

---

[6] A. Samoilovich, "Pervoe tainoe obshchestvo Mlado-Bukhartsev," Vostok no. 1 (1922), pp. 97-99; Sadriddin `Ayniy, Bukhara inqilabi tä'rikhi uchun materiyyallar. Moscow: Khälqlarining Märkäzi Näshriyati, 1926, pp. 65-69; Baymirza Hayit, Turkestan im XX. Jahrhundert. Darmstadt: C. W. Leske Verlag, 1956, pp. 118-120.

Arabiya." In another passage, Mr. `Ayniy commented that `Abdalrauf Fitrat was considered the most gifted and erudite of the Bukharan students (`abdura'of fitrat bukhara oqughuchilari-ning eng iste`dadli ham eng fazili sanalar edi.")"[7]

For the implementation of such cultural programs, the Society for the Education of Children founded two other, related organizations: Ma`rifat, a library and book distributor, which functioned from 1911 to 1917, on the initiative of `Abdalrauf Fitrat, `Osman Khoja, Sadriddin `Ayniy, Sharifjan Mahmud (sic; probably correctly, Mahdum, the name of the highly-placed, moderate judge [qozi] and intellectual, known in literary circles as Sadr-i Ziya), and others.[8] Through the agency of Ma`rifat also came into existence the The Educational Publishing Society of Turan (Turan Nashri Ma`arif Jamiyati), an association intended to publish and disseminate knowledge through the press.[9] That focus upon literacy and publishing nourished a drive in young Mr. Fitrat to teach and write, an aim that would dominate all of his subsequent efforts. Before he achieved wide recognition in

[7] Sädriddin `Äyniy, pp. 69, 88; Edward A. Allworth, "Suppressed Histories of the Jadids in Turkistan and Bukhara," Erling von Mende, ed., Turkestan als historischer Faktor und politische Idee. Festschrift für Baymirza Hayit zu seinem 70. Geburtstag, 17. Dezember 1987. Cologne: Studienverlag, 1988, p. 38.

[8] Timur Kocaoglu, ed., Reform and Revolution in Turkistan, 1900-1924. A Memorial Volume for Osman Khoja. Haarlem, Netherlands: Mehmet Tutuncu, 2000. This armaghan devotes substantial sections to the accomplishments and actions of Osman Khoja, before, during and after he served as President of the nascent Bukharan People's Republic.

[9] Närzullä Yoldashew, pp. 6-7.

his area as a writer and scholar, he served as an instructor in the grammatically deprived populace of Bukhara.[10]

As a student in Istanbul, `Abdalrauf found himself almost penniless. Merely to survive, his poverty forced him to undertake menial work in restaurant kitchens, and the like.[11] Nevertheless, he took advanced study in Madrassah-i Wa`izin, participated in cultural organizations, and occupied himself with putting on paper and publishing the many ideas agitating his fertile mind. In retrospect, the record leaves no doubt about the abundant creative and scholarly productivity of `Abdalrauf Fitrat during his relatively short professional life of 27 years (52 years minus 25, his age when the first known works that he wrote received circulation in print).

As a complement to the sparse biographical information about the personal lives of men such as the Central Asian Reformists, important specimens of each writer/scholar's output usually tell many things about her/his outlook and the prevailing cultural milieu. Consideration of the entire corpus of a prominent cultural and social thinker's works probably can reveal even more about such a person's attitudes, values, ideas, and perhaps much about an individual's background and temperament. This essay aims to create a framework for such a deep study, but not to provide that comprehensive analysis.

---

[10] Hélène Carrère d'Encausse, "Fitrat," <u>The Encyclopaedia of Islam</u>. vol. II (1965), p. 932.

[11] Sewärä Käramätilläkhojäyewä, p. 70.

An interpreter of an author's lifetime of writings, to succeed in the inquiry, must surely understand very much about the mature individual under scrutiny. In his instance, no one can doubt that this Bukharan author and scholar shows the unmistakable traits of a conconformist. Publicly, from early adulthood, he rejected the behavior and ignorance so evident in the religious establishment of his native City. He also spurned the baseless mythology and superstition that permeated much of contemporary religious belief. Through the writings from his Istanbul period he makes clear not only his impatience with the pretensions of incompetent mullahs and imams. Circumspectly, at first, he dissents from the policies of the Bukharan Amir, as well.

Although he found conditions in Bukhara deplorable, 'Abdalrauf Fitrat did not indulge himself in general negativism in his earliest writings from the Istanbul period. In fact, his early published book A Guide for Deliverance (Rähbär-i näjat). #133, dated Petrograd, 1915, offers affirmative advice for attainment of a better life and society. Thus, he combined criticism with constructive proposals. Back in his home City, as well as in Turkistan, he took positive initiatives that helped organize the thinking and activity of Central Asians during the formative period from 1917 to 1923. They included his editing of publications, such as the Samarkand newspaper, Hurriyat, organizing literary circles, notably the Chaghatay Gurungi, preparing publishing ventures with fellow authors, like the pivotal volume of poetic advocacy, Young Uzbek Poets (Ozbek yash sha'irlari) (1922), sending student groups to Europe for modern education, and the like. All of these efforts fell outside the conventions of old Bukhara and of Soviet Bukhara and Turkistan, as well.

With the emergence in Central Asia of strong local Bolshevik forces and their ideology, Mr. Fitrat again shows disagreement by strenuously endeavoring first to influence the direction of policies in the Bukharan People's Conciliar Republic (BPCR) and then satirizing, in writings such as The Judgment Day (Qiyamät), #125, Bolshevik mismanagement of Central Asian affairs. Hoping for his country's political independence and moderation under the new conditions, he affiliated himself temporarily, as did numbers of other intellectuals, with the Bukharan branch of the Communist Party (CP) from 1918 to 1924. In June, 1919, at the CP BPCR's First Congress, members selected him to enter the makeup of the Central Committee CP BPCR. After the overthrow of the Amir, he managed religious philanthropic affairs (waqf) of the Republic (1920-21), successively served as Minister of Foreign Affairs (1922), and of Education (1923) and almost simultaneously as deputy chairman of the Council of Labor of the BPCR (1923). He also worked briefly in the BPCR's ministerial posts for military matters and for finance (1922). (see Figure 2, Bukhara's Final Currency, Bearing the Signature, Fitrat)

B   Competing for Central Asia's Cultural Heart

When the CP branch of the BPCR forced Mr. Fitrat out of office and banished him from Bukhara, in 1923-1924, from Moscow he soon composed and published a series of allegories critiquing obliquely the inhuman behavior, arbitrary notions, and inefficiency of the functionaries and chiefs running the new political system in Bukhara and Turkistan.[12] His ostensibly political sins and nonconformity did not extend to the field of scholarship in general. At the time of his in exile in Russia, he lectured in Moscow's Lazarev Institute of Eastern Languages and then in the Petrograd University Faculty of Oriental Studies.

Immediately afterward, Soviet authorities created hazardous new conditions in the intellectual milieu of Professor Fitrat and his cohorts, in order make Central Asia's cultural and social leaders more manageable for the regime than they had been. The politicians dissolved the supraethnic units of southern Central Asia – the Bukharan People's Conciliar Republic, the Khwarazm People's Conciliar Republic, and the Turkistan Autonomous Soviet Socialist Republic, during 1923-24. In the

---

[12] Baltäbayew, p. 35; "Fiträt," Ozbek sawet entsiklapediyäsi. Tashkent: Ozbek Sawet Entsiklapediyäsi, Bash Redäktsiyäsi, vol. 12 (1979), p. 119; Faizulla Khodzhaev, Izbrannye trudy. Tashkent: Izdatel'stvo "FAN" Uzbekskoi SSR, 1970, vol. 1, p. 455; Dzh. Baibulatov, Chagataizm-Pantiurkizm v uzbekskoi literature. Moscow-Tashkent: Ob'edinenie Gosudarstvennykh Izdatel'stv. Sredneaziatskoe Otdelenie, 1932, pp. 36-37.

following two years they executed the partition of twentieth-century Central Asia along ethnic lines for the first time.

Those actions exerted a huge impact upon the self-aware strata of the population. Such actions removed familiar ground and accepted supraethnic group identities, displaced old lingua francas and altered the outlines of conventional homelands from the lives and concepts of `Abdalrauf Fitrat and his thinking countrymen.

Personally, and rather subtly, he refused to conform to the limitations imposed by those drastic changes. Although every cultural issue now demanded a narrower focus, virtually all of his historical scholarship, as well as new creative writing, insistently reached beyond the contemporary political borders of his assigned administrative unit – the Uzbekistan Soviet Socialist Republic (UzSSR), established 1924-25 – into the broader realms and civilizations of recently bygone eras.

A controversial instance of this dissent brought sharp ideological attacks upon him when he published a literary anthology, entitled Specimens of Uzbek Literature (Ozbek ädäbiyati nämunäläri), #110, (1928) meant for advanced students and adults. The book greatly offended CP critics because it failed to give priority to folklore or to distinguish sufficiently purely Uzbek literature, if such materials yet existed, from broader Central Asian writings. Not only did the compiler not find distinctly Uzbek literature from the past, he refused to pretend that he had found it when the new ideology insisted that he conform.

From his early adulthood, `Abdalrauf Fitrat had shown him-
self to be a convinced internationalist. The ideological conflict
between the realities of Central Asia's cultural history and the
requirements set by the arbitrary ethnic partition of the area's
heritage led to strange charges of "nationalism" against Professor Fitrat (he gained the title of professor beginning in 1924).
Conformity with CP demands on that issue would have obliged
scholars to distort the facts. He could not do it, although others
did not alway stand on principle in this issue. His persistence in
this and related ideas in twentieth-century life of the region led
to disaster during the last phase of his life.

In the Marxist ideologists' drive against the recent past,
`Abdalrauf Fitrat failed to accommodate to the CP's strident
attacks against the Central Asian Reformists (Jadids) of 1900-
1920. He demonstrated his determination to resist censorship in
the last known theatrical work he composed. The authorities
pulled off the scene his last-known theater work, a libretto for
the opera "The Wave" ("Tolqin"), as soon as it received its first
staging in 1936. In it, he evidently offered some dialogue that
avoided castigating the pre-1920 Reformists. That infuriated
ideologists further during a period of savage critical attacks
upon anything that failed to conform slavishly with the propaganda formulas of the CP. One of those prescriptions labeled as
criminal nationalism everything positive having to do with the
pre-Soviet Jadid movement.

To summarize: the chronology of stages in ʿAbdalrauf Fitrat's major nonconformity reach from the beginning to end of his professional career: First, 1911-20, the Istanbul period and Turkistan expatriate disagreement with the religious establishment and government of Bukhara; then, during 1920-23, working against the communists in the Bukharan People's Conciliar Republic and subsequent Bukharan Republic; from 1925 onward, intellectual disagreement with the application of communist theory of national culture to the supraethnic civilization of Central Asia generally and to Uzbekistan, in particular; after the organization of the Writers' Union of the UzSSR in 1932-34 as a powerful political-social monitor, especially, Professor Fitrat still revealed his inability to denigrate or sanitize earlier cultural history, as expected by CP ideologists; and, in particular, the achievements of himself and his Jadid colleagues during the first decades of the century.

In view of these factors, to what extent should readers of ʿAbdalrauf Fitrat's writings regard them as a historical record of the intellectual environment and of the tumultuous years during which he composed them? To respond to that question requires a researcher somehow to measure or estimate the degrees of objectivity or subjectivity apparent in the writings themselves and in the commentaries about them by others, not a simple task.

To complicate matters, this Bukharan author frequently involved himself, intentionally, in misleading or confusing various categories of readers in his audience, especially those regulating morals and ideas from positions of authority. He asserted, during an unpleasant polemic with a communist ideologist, that: "I never in my writings had pretensions against or made claims upon the Soviet Government or the ideology of the Proletariat."[13]

C. `Abdalrauf Fitrat's Writings

The author of the present article has prepared this new Bibliography independently, on the basis of direct examination of numerous works, and, necessarily, on the study of secondary sources. This Bibliography also benefits substantially from valuable lists already published in Central Asia and Turkiye. Uzbekistan's and Tajikistan's scholars in the 1980s and 1990s have started work that allows researchers to test the above proposition through an examination of `Abdalrauf Fitrat's Bibliography. In addition, Central Asian publishers in several republics have reprinted quite a few of Professor Fitrat's earlier, out-of-print, or scarce publications, making them more available for circulation.

Because events resulted in the loss of more than 10 of his writings and of detailed information about them, readers will recognize that dating and establishing the place where he wrote

---

[13] Fiträt, Yapishmägän gäjäklär. Ortaq Baybolätawgä achiq khät," in Näim Kärimaw, Erik Kärimaw, Sheräli Turdiew, compilers, *Chin sewish*, p. 245.

many of the early works not only raises difficulty but serious doubt concerning published information. Secondary sources, upon which these retrospective surveys must rely, repeatedly disagree with one another. A current Uzbek author has summed up this dilemma in the effort to determine the sequence and dating of `Abdalrauf Fitrat's writings: "the dating of the [lost] plays "Blood" (`Qan'), #122, and `Beggijan', #20, as early as 1917-1918 is unsubstantiated."[14] To make the point, that author cites an article by Qayyum Ramazan – a participant in the Chaghatay Gurungi, the literary discussion circle established by Mr. Fitrat in 1918 – and published under the penname Oktam in June 1924. In it, Oktam comments that "Qan" had been written recently (yängi yazilghan), perhaps as late as 1923 or 1924. However, an eye- witness said to the author of this essay that he had read the draft of an unfinished play, entitled "Sacred Blood" (Muqäddäs qan) or simply "Blood," by `Abdalrauf Fitrat, proba- bly the work referred to by Qayyum Ramazan as "Qan." The witness dated his experience during the existence of the Chaghatay Gurungi, in which the he was permitted by the group's leader to sit in its gatherings as a novice observer. Bolshevik authorities banned that organization in 1922.[15] Mr.

---

[14] Shuhrät Rizäew, Jädid drämäsi. Tashkent: "Shärq" Näshriyat-Mätbää Kontsernining Bash Tähririyäti, 1997, p. 115.

[15] Edward Allworth, Uzbek Literary Politics. The Hague: Mouton & Co., 1964, p. 217, n.6.

Fitrat may have completed this play later, but he evidently wrote a version of it before the end of 1922.

Problems arise not only in the dating of `Abdalrauf Fitrat's lost works, but in fixing the chronology for some of those available in print. An accomplished Japanese scholar has convincingly established the date for the publication of `Abdalrauf's early work, ...The Dispute... (...Munozira...), #97. His study dates it as H. malî 1327, that is, A.D.1911-12.[16] This clarification explains the apparent tension between the year of the young Bukharan's arrival in 1910 to study in Istanbul, and the 1909 issue date conventionally, and, it now seems, incorrectly, assigned for publication of that initial work.

With such warnings in mind, readers will understand that definitive dating of every piece of writing by Mr. Fitrat remains incomplete until further documentation from the files and archives of Central Asia, the Central Asian emigration, and other sources, can offer convincing proof of the chronologies.

Table 1, below, divides `Abdalrauf Fitrat's productive life into three segments, defined mainly by political developments and related cultural and social affairs: a. the rise of Reformist activism early in the twentieth century and the collapse of the Czarist government and state in March 1917, the establishment of the Turkistan Autonomous Soviet Socialist Republic in 1918, the decline of the Bukharan Amirate and the Khivan Khanate; b.

---

[16] Hisao Komatsu, 20. Yüzyil bashlarinda Orta Asya'da Türkçülük ve devrim hareketleri. Ankara: Turhan Kitabevi Yayinlari, 1993, pp. 5-8.

the replacement of those dynastic states by "peoples" republics in 1920 and the activation of the Uzbekistan SSR and, within it, the Tajikistan Autonomous Soviet Socialist Republic in 1924-1925, along with the outlawing of confessional schools around 1927; and, c. the relentless purges of intellectuals and other leaders of Central Asian society begun in the 1920s but intensifying notably during 1937-38.

His range of subjects during each of these three periods (9, 7 and 11 years, respectively) relates to the evolution in his interests and focus, but also connects with his Bukharan background, his public life as student and adult during the cultural, political and social changes in which he functioned during successive periods. Above all, the breadth of interests demonstrates the extraordinary scale of 'Abdalrauf Fitrat's intellectual and esthetic concerns.

Table 1, below, reveals a predictable pattern showing that 'Abdalrauf Fitrat wrote largely about culture and politics during all three periods. Unsurprising, because he moved mainly in the realm of literature and education, though he participated actively, throughout the first two periods, in the political life of his Bukharan homeland. The record of political writings inversely mirrors the intensification of government repression under Czarist and Soviet conditions and the stifling of public dissent and discussion.

From a count of 28 booklets and articles that appeared in the period just before the onset of complete Soviet dominance in

Bukhara and Turkistan, his political output dwindled to nine writings between 1920 and 1926, and only two during the decade following.

The quantity of his writings (largely published) in the fields of culture underwent no comparable decrease. Forty-nine appeared during the seven years after 1919, and 50 in the period from 1927 through 1937. Although hard-line Marxists sharply accused him of straying into political deviation in a number of the works he composed or published from 1927 onward, readers in a democratic society would hardly have regarded as political his articles and books about culture composed in those years.

The growth in his cultural publishing seems to indicate that conditions deprived 'Abdalrauf Fitrat of the political arena that served him in the Jadid years between 1909 and 1919 and the brief life-span of the Bukharan Peoples' Conciliar Republic (1920-1924). Thereafter, he necessarily swung away from the field of politics after the establishment, in late 1924 and early 1925, of those truly Soviet creations – the Uzbekistan Soviet Socialist Republic and the Tajikistan Autonomous Soviet Socialist Republic.

Unlike the reduction in numbers of political writings, the quantity of works regarding religion reflected another turn in Sovietizing Central Asia. Beginning around 1927, five anti-religious publications appeared under Professor Fitrat's name, nearly equalling his output of writings positively concerned with religion before 1920. A striking disappearence of published work about social problems and reforms after 1919 showed the loss of safe opportunities for opening free discussions respecting any aspect of social and political life other than acceptance of the official agenda and the specified Soviet viewpoint. This surely put an end to the open questioning and skepticism found in much of Professor Fitrat's earlier writing.

The sudden intensification of restrictions on press freedom jerked him in two directions. He apparently contrived stories and other writings superficially resembling anti-religious propaganda "The Ascension" ("Me'raj"), #92, and "Zähra's Faith" ("Zähraning imani"), #189, for example). On the other hand, he entirely refrained from expressing his political views openly in print. All of his "religious" writings published after 1926 fit into that classification.[17] In contrast, writings about religious poets and teachers such as Ahmad Yassawiy (d.1166) – "Ahmad Yassawiy" ("Ahmäd yäsäwi"), #9, and "Inquiries Concerning Poets of the Yassawiy School," ("Yasawi maktabi sha`irlari toghrisida tekshirishlar"), #180, in Table 1 and in the Bibliography – that treat religion as a facet of Central Asian civilization, belong here in the sphere of Culture.

This Bukharan author's literary works in many instances carried a strong social and cultural message, one with significant political undertones. Detachment seldom attracted him, but

---

[17] See Khudasizlar (Samarkand) nos. 1, 2, 4, 5, 6 (1928), nos. 2/3 (1930). For locations of several of these, see Edward Allworth, Nationalities of the Soviet East: Publications and Writing Systems. New York: Columbia University Press, 1971, p. 193.

his objectivity never seemed to waver in the serious scholarship that made his academic reputation. The style of committed writing, common in Reformist literature, seems subjective. His approach to themes and substance may sometimes deserve the label subjective, but he did not juggle the facts, preferring to use reason even in polemics, such as those prompted by extremely adverse ideological criticism. These writings evidently aroused the suspicious antagonism of ideologists even more than the overtly political tracts. The methodology employed to organize Table 1 allocates such ostensibly tendentious works to Culture, not to Politics.

'Abdalrauf Fitrat's political writings appeared frequently during the short life of the Bukharan Peoples' Conciliar Republic from 1920 to 1923-24 or shortly before its establishment. See the title Politics of the East (Shärq siyasäti), ##145-46, dated 1919-1920/1921, for example. That same period saw the publication of his play preoccupied with the political weakness and failure of the last Ashtarkhanid (i.e., Janid) dynastic ruler of Bukhara, 'Abul Fayz Khan ('Abul Fayz Khan), #2, ostensibly the Bukharan Amirate's sovereign from 1711 to 1747, though the rising power of the Manghit chieftains really directed affairs of State. The Bibliography classifies this drama under Culture rather than Politics in the Synchronic Presentation. In the final years, Professor Fitrat's writings, now known, directly treated politics only twice, in a dynastic history of the Manghit rulers who succeeded the Ashtarkhanids, he wrote Amir Alimkhan's

Reign (Davra-i hukmronii amir olimkhon), #39, in Tajik in 1930.

He offered a strong rebuttal in 1929 under a clever title, "Unsnarable Tangles," ("Yäpishmägän gäjäklär"), #179, to an adversary who forced a wide-ranging defense upon him. A CP ideologist of Central Asia, J. Baybulataw, politically attacked many of his writings.[18] By that time, avoiding explicit political affairs, Professor Fitrat also wrote almost no articles or books devoted specifically to the economy, and focused an inconsequential number openly on social problems.

An examination of the corpus of known writings attributable to `Abdalrauf Fitrat reveals his consistent preoccupation with alphabet reform, history, language, literary history, literature and poetics throughout his shortened adult life. Open concern for social issues such as family and schooling receives much greater emphasis in the decade before 1920 than later, but the Soviet, class-oriented policies regarding them can explain his reticence to pursue those issues after 1919. The same must apply to the author's withdrawal from public discussion of general political issues and ideology, as such, after 1923. Though he wrote actively about the contemporary politics of 1917, in "The Election Neared" ("Säylaw yäqinläshdi"), #142, among other articles, he evidently judged that voting manipulated by Soviet politicians could not merit his public attention, for none

[18] Dzh. Baibulatov, Chagataizm-pantiurkizm v uzbekskoi literature. Moscow-Tashkent: OGIZ, Sredneaziatskoe Otdelenie, 1932.

of his published works known to this researcher analyzes the later, single-slate balloting in the USSR.

At some risk, Professor Fitrat did write a significant article, "What Must We Do about the Old Parochial Schools?" ("Eski mäktäblärni nimä qilish keräk?"), #43, about the drastic fate overtaking Islamic institutions of Central Asia by 1927. Soviet leaders ordered them closed. This action provoked a furious response from pious Central Asians. A former minister in the 1917 government of the Qoqan (Khokand) Autonomy, Nasir Khan Tora Kamalkhan Torayew, in the late 1920s and early 1930s actively fought against Soviet anti-religious measures with various actions, including anonymous letters denouncing the CP's atheistic policies. In 1930, one handbill declared "At present, no madrassahs, no darwish cloister (khanaqah), no religious schools, no religious judges, no Muslim legal experts (muftis), no seminary teachers (mudärrises), and no spiritual instructors remain in Central Asia."[19]

That response immediately drew the attention of the forerunner to the infamous Soviet Committee for State Security (KGB), then called the United State Political Administration (Ob'edinennoe Gosudarstvennoe Politicheskoe Upravlenie (OGPU). Soviet authorities attempted to link the former Reformists with this militant resistance led by the Qorbashis in southern Central

[19] Reinhard Eisener, trans. and introduction, Konterrevolution af dem Lande. Zur inneren Sicherheitslage in Mittelasien 1929-1930 aus der Sicht der OGPU. Berlin: Das Arabische Buch. ANOR, no. 6, 1999, pp. 62-64, 110f.

Asia as late as the early 1930s. Though some aims espoused by the Jadids resembled those of the Qorbashis, Reformists such as Professor Fitrat generally neither advocated violence nor the revival of the Amirate of Bukhara or of the Islamic parochial school system that had functioned before 1920 or up to 1927.[20]

Equally distressing to educators of the region, official communist atheism blotted out or strongly diminished thoughtful discussion about humanistic educational policy. After 1920, they could no longer openly debate the desirable forms, content, practice and symbols of religion and religious enlightenment in Central Asia. This deprived intellectuals such as `Abdalrauf Fitrat of the free press needed for informed public interaction or commentary about a belief system still at the core of the population's beliefs and outlook.

D.   Periodization

The following compilation, Table 1, "A Synchronic Presentation of `Abdalrauf Fitrat's Writings, 1911-1937," serves two main purposes: it offers at a glance a chronological and statistical summary of the subsequent Bibliography. Perhaps equally

---

[20] Edward A. Allworth, The Modern Uzbeks. From the Fourteenth Century to the Present. A Cultural History. Stanford: The Hoover Institution, 1993, 3d printing, p. 176.

important in this presentation, Table 1 serves as a general subject index to that Bibliography.

The method of analysis sorts his entire output of writings into five broad subject categories:

1. Culture includes alphabets and orthography, art; biography, books and manuscripts, drama and theater, education and schools, ethhics, fiction, games and celebrations (other than religious), grammar and language, history and history of science, institutions and associations, literacy, literary and cultural history, literature, music, orthography, philosophy, poetics, poetry, writing systems;

2. Economy relates to agriculture, farming, finance, food, irrigation, land tenure, slave owning, trade;

3. Politics includes constitution, discrimination, elections and voting, government and administration, ideology, the military and war, nationality, national identity, oppression, parties, policies, political history, reforms.

4. Religion embraces atheism, Christianity, faith, intolerance, Islam, madrassahs, mosques, mullahs, myths, other religions, sacred texts, sufism, superstition.

5. Society includes children's upbringing, drug addiction, family, human qualities, polygamy, slavery, social conditions, women's and workmen's status, youths.

The author of the present monograph has assigned these writings to subject categories and calculated the totals and percentages of Professor Fitrat's writings registered in the Bibliography. More than 36.6 percent of these titles appeared during his initial period of authorship, 1911-1919. Another 30.9 percent came in the following years, 1920-1926; and, 32.5 percent fall into his final decade, 1927-1937. Although the early years produced the greatest number of titles, the author's output remained remarkably steady throughout his career. Altogether: 191 titles during 27 years = 7.07 works annually, on average.

Throughout the working life of `Abdalrauf Fitrat, in quantity, the heading of Culture far outweighs the other subject areas, with 123 titles, 64.4 percent of the subjects, not surprising, considering Professor Fitrat's vocation as teacher, literary historian and creative writer. Perhaps more unexpected in the survey, during the first period, Politics surpassed Culture, numerically, and, overall, came second after Culture, with 39 titles, that is, 20.4 percent of subject matter. Nearly all of these political writings appeared during the period when he engaged himself very actively in responsibilities relating to the Reformist (Jadid) movement, the Young Bukharan political party, and the Government of the Bukharan People's Conciliar Republic. Opportunities for continuing political analysis and argument nearly disappeared during the dangerous years, 1927-1937 of heavy CP control over culture and society.

The analytical method employed here places all poetry and fiction in the category of culture, regardless of the didacticism or political content of much of this poetry and creative prose. A more refined categorization of each entry, particularly for the

newspaper articles and unpublished manuscripts, must wait
until some great research center or library assembles all of the
writer/scholar's compositions in one collection for convenient
access and close comparison in the study of students and other
researchers.

Table 1. A Synchronic Presentation of `Abdalrauf Fitrat's Writ-
ings, 1911-1937[21] (The numbers listed in dated columns
designate the entries in the Bibliography given below. An
asterisk* marks dating provisionally estimated for about
15 undated writings)

Subjects	1911-19	1920-26	1927-37
Culture	1, 10, 18, 20,	2, 6, 8, 11,	3, 4, 5, 7, 9,
(total 123)	60, 61*, 71,	13, 15, 19,	14, 31, 32,
	80, 82, 84,	21,22, 25,	35*, 38, 40*,
	93, 97, 99,	30, 34, 36,	41, 42, 43,
	103, 107,	47, 50, 52*,	44*, 45, 46,
	122, 140,	56, 73, 75,	51, 57, 59,
	141, 151,	77, 81*, 85,	68*, 79, 86,
	159, 163,	88, 89, 92,	90*, 94, 96,
	164, 174,	98, 100, 101,	105, 110,
	190	102, 104,	111, 112,

---

[21] Sources: See below, the "Bibliography of Works by `Abdalrauf Rahim-oghli
Fitrat. An Alphabetical, Annotated Listing."

		106, 116, 117, 118, 119, 120, 123, 125, 130, 136, 137, 143, 144, 148, 149, 150, 171, 177	113, 114, 115, 121, 127, 131, 134, 135, 138, 139, 147, 153, 157, 158, 165, 167, 173, 175, 180, 188
Economy (6)	17, 172		108*, 109*, 155*, 166
Politics (39)	23, 24, 27, 39, 49, 55, 58, 62, 63, 64, 67, 69, 70, 83, 95, 124, 142, 145, 154, 156, 157*, 162, 168, 169, 170, 178, 183, 187	74, 76, 78, 146, 158*, 161*, 176*, 182*, 186	33, 179
Religion	28, 87, 129,	160	12, 91, 126,

(13)	132, 133, 152, 185		189, 191
Society (10)	16, 26, 29, 48*, 53, 54, 65, 72, 184		128
Total	70 titles	59 titles	62 titles

These findings may suggest that numbers of his writings did not directly treat the panorama of Bukharan life up to 1937. But the pattern in his whole body of works – with their omissions as well as emphases – surely reflects the exigencies of the Bukharan and larger Central Asian ordeal under successive absolutist rulers and dictators from 1911 through 1937.

E.   Previous Lists

Other scholars have compiled and printed (none in English, evidently) at least three separate extensive inventories of `Abdalrauf Fitrat's titles. They overlap but do not entirely coincide. In that process, these scholars have also supplied some additional bibliographical information about his works. In chronological order, the first of the three lists, organized by broad subjects and published in 1990, notes 90 separate titles in 9 categories: verse, prose fiction, dramas, social works, translations, linguistics, literary theory, literary history, culture of the

East, and music history and theory.[22] Besides those writings that received publication, in the article introducing that list the compiler comments about the loss of several works that the Soviet government censors, or the press and publishing houses, apparently refused to issue, owing to the negative political profile Marxist ideologists gave to Professor Fitrat in the late 1920s and 1930s.[23]

The compiler of a second inventory of `Abdalrauf Fitrat's writings, aided by an associate, in 1994 issued a longer list, of 134 titles, arranged in chronological order of publication or, if not published, with date of composition, if known. Like the 1990 inventory, this second list included some unpublished works. Unlike the earlier one, it named some translations into Russian from author Fitrat's published work.[24] Most valuable for students and other researchers: the compilers of that second inventory indicate after many of the titles the institute, library or other location in the former USSR where readers can find a large percentage of these publications.

The most extensive list yet compiled of `Abdalrauf Fitrat's works has appeared in Turkish in the intensive research of a Turkish scholar under the title, Fitrat and His Works (1997),

---

[22] Hämidullä Baltäbayew, 1990, pp. 38-39.

[23] ibid., pp. 36-37.

[24] Ilham Ghäniyew, Fiträtning trägediyä yärätish mäharäti (Managräfiyä). Tashkent: Ghäfur Ghulam namidägi Ädäbiyat wä Sän'ät Näshriyati, 1994, pp. 135-145.

which attributes additional entries to the Central Asian author.[25]
This compilation, presents the titles of works written in
Turki/Uzbek in two major divisions: A. Books and Tracts; B.
Articles. Subdivisions: poems; stories; plays; writings about
music; writings about language; literary theory; history, culture
and literary history; translations; other writings (largely
political-social). Under the second main heading "Articles," the
scholar has organized his list according to the periodical or
book titles in which 'Abdalrauf Fitrat's contributions appear,
beginning with Hurriyät (July 1917) and ending with Ozbek
sawet ädäbiyati No. 10 (1936). In Hurriyät, which 'Abdalrauf
edited beginning with issue no. 27, the compiler of list Tl, Yar.
Doc. Dr. Yusuf Avci, has uncovered by far the largest number
of articles, 39 all told, written by 'Abdalrauf Fitrat and published in one newspaper. French scholars have called that newspaper, published by the Zarafshan Society, "for the epoch, the
most influential, best executed, and most interesting of the Jadids' journals of Turkistan."[26]

Despite the care with which scholars compile inventories
such as the three preceding the present one, it remains likely
that later inquiries will identify a few additional writings, or that
some researcher will discover lists compiled, perhaps by ideo-

---

[25] Yusuf Avci, Fitrat ve eserleri. Ankara: T.C. Kültür Bakanligi, 1997, pp. 109-117.

[26] Alexandre Bennigsen and Chantal Lemercier-Quelquejay, La Presse et le
mouvement national chez les Musulmans de Russie avant 1920. Paris: Mouton & Co.,
1964, p. 267.

logical critics, secret police, or censors, during the life of Professor Fitrat, himself.

For now, however, the present Bibliography, from direct de visu examination and additional study of secondary materials, enlarges the list and also combines the information found in the previous three inventories. Scholars and other readers may wish to regard this Synchronic Presentation and Bibliography as a new working catalog of `Abdalrauf Rahim-oghli Fitrat's writings, and one that probably lists most of his works. Even so, it will very likely undergo amplification and correction in future.

This research entailed the scanning of relevant books, encyclopedic entries, and available issues and tables of contents for periodicals published during the second and third decades and at least the start of the fourth decade (1911-1930s) of the twentieth century – the years in which most of Professor Fitrat's writings appeared. Periodicals systematically surveyed to the exent that U.S.A. collections hold them: Alängä, Ayinä, Bukhara akhbari, Inqilab, Khudasizlar, Mä`arif wä oqutghuchi, Rahbar-i donish. For the same purpose, other researchers (see the Bibliography, below) have scanned some or all of Bukhara-yi shärif, Hurriyät (Samarkand), Ishtirakiyun, Ortä asiya ädäbiyati and Qizil ozbekistan issued up to the end of Professor Fitrat's publishing history.

In each case in which Professor Fitrat's writings appeared in book form or in periodicals or symposia, the compiler of this Bibliography enters full information if the work has become accessible to him. For separate publications, that entry includes the work's full title, place of publication, publisher's name, date of publication, number of pages in the separate book or booklet, sometimes, number of copies printed. For journal and symposium articles that the compiler has consulted directly, the entries include article title, title of periodical, newspaper or collection of articles, the issue number for a journal, date of publication, inclusive page numbers for the article, sometimes the place of publication.

Entries representing works not yet consulted directly will offer all of the same information, if a search turns it up, but in many instances the secondary sources fail to record full titles, publishers' names or numbers of pages, for example. The compiler regrets the necessity to refer to secondary sources for a number of the titles. Without doubt, no library in the world yet holds a complete collection of `Abdalrauf Fitrat's writings, but scholars may hope that this list will facilitate research and collection-building in libraries and centers focused upon the history of modern Bukhara and Central Asia generally.

The transliteration systems followed here for the various alphabets, with slight modifications (w instead of v in Uzbek, for example), appear in Nationalities of the Soviet East. Publications and Writing Systems. New York: Columbia University Press, 1971. The list of indexed publications in that same book includes a number of titles by `Abdalrauf Fitrat. The compiler has rendered transliterations directly from the original, usually without attempting to standardize or correct spellings found in the publications listed. In one exception to that rule, for those titles drawn from Turkish List No. 1 (T1), the transliteration used here has reverted, as accurately as possible without examining the original, to Turki/Uzbek from the Turkish spellings and usages introduced in T1. Entries lacking the sign T1 or the coding explained immediately below represent information drawn from personal inspection of publications by the compiler of this work or from reliable secondary sources other than those in U1 (Baltabayew), U2 (Ghaniyew), B1 (Yoldashew) or T1 (Avci).

In this Bibliography (U1) designates Uzbekistan List No. 1 (1990), prepared by Hamidulla Baltabayew, as a source, but not necessarily the sole source for an entry so marked; (U2) specifies Uzbekistan List No. 2 (1994), prepared by Ilham Ghaniyew and B. Ergashew, as a source, but not necessarily the exclusive source for information in the entry. The code B1 indicates information from Narzulla Yoldashew's essay (1996) introducing the new edition of selections from 'Abdalrauf Fitrat's Guide to Salvation (Rähbär-i näjat), #133, listed below.

At the end of an entry in the present Bibliography, in those instances when the compiler can show the present location in North America of a work or a microform or xerographic copy of it, readers will observe the following U.S. Marc Code List symbols: for Columbia University libraries: (NNC); for the Library of Congress: (DLC); for The New York Public Library: (NN);

for McGill University Library in Montreal: (CaQMM). For titles located in libraries outside North America, in Europe and the Middle East, the Bibliography will provide the name of a library that preserves `Abdalrauf Fitrat's work, if he knows that information. As noted above, the footnotes to Ilham Ghaniyew's list in his book Fitrat's Great Mastery of Creating Tragedy (Fiträtning trägediyä yärätish mäharäti) (1994), supply the locations in the former USSR for many of `Abdalrauf Fitrat's writings.

F.   An Assessment and Acknowledgement

Evaluating the writings of an author, such as `Abdalrauf Fitrat, presents real difficulties. He engaged in educating people while simultaneously trying to outwit the political ideologists and to persuade the general public and its leadership to agree with his own ideas and principles.

From that standpoint, the character and number of extant publications written or edited by him and available for study affords researchers the opportunity to look for patterrns in `Abdalrauf Fitrat's creative, scholarly and journalistic legacy. Versatile as the body of work appears, owing to its idiosyncrasies, its selectivity and what seems a great degree of personal viewpoint, rather than universality, the writings probably possesses the comprehensiveness to qualify them as a reliable mirror closely reflecting the author's times and places. He played a leading role, and the legacy of his writings already accessible should give a basis for judging the presence or absence of bias in them. And, they give evidence that certain categories of the works – surely the scholarship and translation – deserve the label "objective."

ʿAbdalrauf Fitrat's individuality reveals itself in his selection of scholarly problems to solve and in his approach to social and cultural causes. His scope hugely broadened, from the confines of what he knew as his Bukharan homeland, to encompass all Turkistan. In his day, very few Central Asians qualified as deeply erudite and broadly educated at the same time. His many serious studies of Chaghatay and Turki, Persian and Tajik culture and literature confirm this. Exactly this breadth of knowledge and cultural vision provoked the animosity of the new ideologists demanding that educators, as well as the educated, regard the world only through the narrow, lower-class outlook of the mainly illiterate local proletariat.

Unable to conform to that requirement, his dissent expresses itself frequently in his own literary efforts. Subtle wit and great intelligence combined to supply many possibilities to display ʿAbdalrauf Fitrat's versatility. According to a retrospective acknowledgement by a hostile critic in 1936, Professor Fitrat succeeded in "tweaking and stinging" Soviet authorities while entertaining the Central Asian reading public and theater goers with his numerous literary and dramatic offerings.[27] Such intellectual audacity required a person with just the attributes of this talented man.

Two types of the author's writings reflect closely the evolution of Central Asian cultural and sometimes political history. To the extent that the writings treated topical material, of course, scholars must regard them as timely. More abstract, but of greater import, the writings dealing with contemporary ideas and conflicts provide a significant barometer

of the fluctuations changing cultural and social history.

Starting actively in the early-to-mid-1920s, the great controversy, mentioned above, over the place of the rich, old, Central Asian cultural heritage in public education of the 1920s and 1930s, grew more rancorous as years went by. Political ideologists rejected any suggestion that it could serve as an appropriate matter for treatment in a communist history published or taught in the contemporary era. The arguments over this question engaged Professor Fitrat's convictions profoundly. For that reason, strict Marxist ideologists could not tolerate most of his large body of research and academic writing. His studies of medieval Central Asian literature, such as Knowledge that Brings Bliss (Qutadgu bilig), #130, and the anthologies of texts – The Earliest Turki Literature... (Eng eski turk adabiyati...),

---

[27] Hämid Älimjan. "Fiträtning ädäbiy ijadi häqidä," <u>Uch tamlik tänlängän äsärlär</u>. Tashkent: OzSSR Däwlät Bädiiy Ädäbiyat Näshriyati, 1960, vol. 3, p. 244.

#41 – for example, drawn from that great heritage, seemed to codify his refusal to accept Soviet guidelines.

In good part, his personal activity as a Reformist during the decades before 1920 also began to make him an outcast in the new political culture. Soviet managers soon connected the old heritage with the Jadid phenomenon. Attacks upon Jadidism, as Russians called it, caught up Professor Fitrat and his colleagues into a net cast for all older intellectuals.

The very narrowness of the prescriptions issued by Marxist ideologists made impossible his continued participation in the cultural activity of the Uzbekistan SSR. By 1937, the Soviet ideologists had effectively banned the publishing and performance of his writings. Nevertheless, as the posthumous reevaluation and reprinting of many of his writings has shown in the 1980s and 1990s, his works have lasting value and special meaning in societies starved for self-expression under continuing, harsh dictatorships. In that respect, Professor Fitrat made a splendid contribution to the latest cultural history and, perhaps, a renewal of his political ideas among younger intellectuals of Tajikistan and Uzbekistan today.

Not only the sheer number of writings, but their quality merits comment; and, perhaps even more deserving of attention, the breadth of the author's fields of interest, from chess to irrigation, drug addiction to classical Central Asian music. Many of his studies appeared in early stages of modern indigenous scholarship regarding Central Asia, yet they remain seminal in present-day research. Others laid the groundwork for much of the later inquiry. Twenty-first century students and researchers treating the culture and society of Bukhara and Turkistan as well as their successors, Tajikistan and Uzbekistan, may disregard few of Professor Fitrat's original studies. Literary and social historians interested in southern Central Asia's culture and people during the first three decades of the twentieth century may not safely ignore the works of poet and creative writer `Abdalrauf Fitrat.

Besides the respect due `Abdalrauf Fitrat for the formidable patrimony he left to present-day researchers, scholars and students in this field owe special gratitude to Candidate in Philological Studies, Hamidulla Baltabayew, who pioneered in the effort to compile the first extensive, published list of `Abdalrauf Fitrat's written works.[28] Thanks go, also in Uzbekistan, to Dr. Ahmad Aliyew, B. Ergashew, Dr. Sadir Erkinaw, Ilham Ghaniyew, Professor Majid Hasanaw, Dr. Begali Qasimaw, Docent K. Shadmanaw, Dr. Sherali Turdiyew, and to Docent Narzulla Yoldashew, and others; in Europe and the U.S.A, to Yar.Doc. Dr. Yusuf Avci, Prof. Dr. Ingeborg Baldauf, Prof. Hélène Carrère d'Encausse, Stéphane A. Dudoignon, as well as Dr. Baymirza Hayit, Prof. Adeeb Khalid and Prof. Timur Kocaoglu, for the important contributions they have made to the study of

---

[28] Hämidullä Baltäbayew, 1990, pp. 34-39

`Abdalrauf Fitrat's biography and writings and his important place in Central Asia's recent history.

II.   BIBLIOGRAPHY OF WORKS BY `ABDALRAUF RAHIM-OGHLI FITRAT

An Alphabetical, Annotated Listing (for subject headings, see numbers in Table 1, above)

1. Äbu (Äba) muslim. Alti-pärdäli fäji`ä 1916 (unpublished).

2. Äbul fäyz khan. Bukhara olkäsining tarikhidan. Besh pärdälik faji`ä. Moscow: SSSR Khälqlärining Märkäz Näshriyati, 1924, 92 pp., 5,000 copies. See also Shärq yulduzi no. 1 (1989) and XX asr ozbek adabiyati (majmua) (1993), compiled by N. Kärimaw, et al, pp. 54-77. Another edition came out in Chin sewish (1996), pp. 39-75. (NN)

3. "Äbulkasim Firdavsii," Sotsialistik fan wa tekhnika (Sotsialisticheskaia nauka i tekhnika) nos. 10/11 (1934),

pp. 1-19. In Russian.

4. (U1) "Äbulqasim Firdawsiy," Ozbekistan shora adabiyati nos. 7/8 (1934).

5. (U1) "Äbulqasim Firdawsii zamani wa muhiti," Ozbek sawet adabiyati, No. 10 (1936).

6. "Achchighlanma degan eding?" Ozbek yash sha`irlari... (1922), pp. 6-7. (Lunds Universitetsbibliotek and NN)

7. (U2) (with Atajan Hashimaw) "Adäbiy meras wä chighätay ädäbiyati," Qizil ozbekistan July 16, 17, (1929).

8. Ädäbiyat qa`idalari. Tashkent: Ozbekistan Däwlät Näshriyati, 1926, 122 pp., 3,000 copies. Reissued in a new edition prepared by Hämidullä Baltäbayew, in 1995, 112 pp., 10,000 copies. (DLC and NN – reprint only)

9. "Ähmäd yäsäwi," Mä`arif wä oqutghuchi no. 6 (1927), pp. 29-33; ibid., nos. 7/8 (1927), pp. 39-43. (DLC and NN)

10. "Ähwal-i hazirä," Hurriyät no. 85 (April ? 1918).

11. (U2) "Äjayib ortälik," Ortä asiya ädäbiyati (Nov. 21, 1933).

Ämir alimkhanning hukmranlik däwri. (see Davra-i hukumronii amir olimkhon, below)

12. (U2) Ana tili. Darslik, coauthored with Shaqirjan Rahimiy and Qayum Ramazan. Tashkent 1918.

13. "Aq mazar," Khudasizlar no. 6 (August 1928), pp. 40-44. (DLC and NN)

14. Arslan. Burunghi Bukhara khanlighida yashaghan dihqanlar hayatidan alinghan. Besh pärdälik dramma. [dedication printed on title page:] "Jumhuriyätimiz tamanidan muwffäqiyat [sic] häm `ädalät bilän ijra itlmäkdä [sic] bolghan yir islahatigha baghislaymän." Samarkand-Tashkent: Ozbekistan Däwlät Näshriyati, 1926, 119 pp., 4,000 copies. Ozbekistan ädäbiyati wä sän`äti reissued the first scene from the play on Dec. 11, 1987, p. 3. A complete new edition of Arslan came out in Tashkent 70

years after the first publication. See Chin sewish (1996), pp.
164-236. (DLC and NN)

15. Äruz häqidä. Tashkent: Fanlar Komiteti Nashriyati, 1936.
Reissued in a new edition prepared by Hamidulla Baltabayew,
Tashkent: "Oqituwchi," 1997, 80 pp., 3,000 copies. (NN reprint
only)

16. "Awunchaq," Ozbek yash sha`irlari... (1922), pp. 8-9.
(Lunds Universitetsbibliotek and NN)

17. (B1) Ayilä (wäzifä-i khanädari). Baku: Mirza Abdulwa-
hid Munzim, 1916 (in Tajik).

18. (U2) "Azuq mäsäläsi," Hurriyät (Aug. 15, 1917).

19. Bedil. Mir mäjlisdä. Moscow: Millät Ishläri Kämisärligi
qashida "Märkäzi Shärq Näshriyati," Dec. 15, 1923/24, 54 pp.,
5,000 copies. The Moscow publishing house for the Soviet East
here follows the old orthography for Central Asian texts printed
in the unmodified Arabic script, largely devoid of vowel signs
in medial position. Inconsistently, it prints mlt for millät, mrkzi
for märkäzi, and the like. In this case, the compiler supplies the
missing vowel signs. (NN)

20. Beggijan (Bekjan) p'yesäsi. Besh pärdäli faj`iä. n.p.:
written 1920. Evidently unpublished and text yet undiscovered.
But (U2) in footnote 26, p. 139, cites information suggesting
that the play received publication in 1920: Tamashächi,
"Begijan," Mehnätkäshlär tawushi (Samarkand) (March 27,
1920).

21. "Behbodining saghanasini izlädim," Ozbek yash sha'ir-lari... (1922), pp. 18-19. (T1) Reprinted in Fän wä turmish no. 1 (1989). (Lunds Universitetsbibliotek and NN)

22. "Bir az kul!" Ozbek yash sha'irlari... (1922), pp. 5-6. (NNC and NN)

23. (U2 and T1) "Birinchi charämiz," Hurriyät no. 34 (Aug. 29, 1917).

24. Boyonat-i sayyoh-i hindi. Dar al-Khilafat: Hikmat, 1330 [1911/12], 128 pp. In Tajik. Trans. to Russian by A. N. Kondrat'ev and published as Razskazy indiiskago puteshestvennika. Bukhara kak ona est': Samarkand: Mullah Behbudiy, 1913, 111 pp. Also issued in Uzbek translation in Shärq yulduzi No. 3 (1991). (NN)

25. (U2 and T1) "Bu kun," Hurriyät no. 37 (Sept. 7, 1917).

26. (T1) "Bukhara khanlighida achlik," Hurriyät no. 53 (Dec. ? 1917).

27. "'Bukhara, khivä, rosyä' munasabäti tä'rikhiyäläri," Mä'arif wä oqutghuchi no. 2 (1925), p. 95. (DLC and NN)

28. (T1) "Bukhara ulemasi," Hurriyät no. 48 (Oct. 31, 1917).

29. (U1) "Bukhara yashlari haqida," Ulugh turkistan (May 30, 1918).

30. (T1) "Bukharada inqilab," Hurriyät nos. 69, 72, 75 (? ? 1918).

31. (U1) "Bukharada inqilab tarikhi" (prepared wih Sadriddin 'Ayniy but unfinished).

32. (U2 and T1) "Bukharaning askari," Hurriyät no. 32 (Aug. 23, 1917) and (Sept. 29, 1917).

33. (T1) "Bukharaning hali," Hurriyät no. 62 (Jan. ? 1918).

34. "Chighatay ädäbiyati," Qizil qalam majmu`asi. Samarkand-Tashkent: Ozbekistan Däwlät Näshriyati, 1929, vol. 2, pp. 25-32. (NN)

35. Chin sewish. Hind ikhtilalchilari turmishindan alingan 5 pardali ishqiy hissiy faji`adir. Calligraphy throughout by `Abdalqadir Murad. [Also printed on title page:] "Nashriyat-i ghazi yonisning tortinchisi." Tashkent: Ghazi Yonis, 1920, 47 pp. ; and, a new, full transliteration into Cyrillic appeared in Chin Sewish. Hind ikhtilalchiläri turmushidän alinghan besh pärdäli ishqiy-hissiy fajiadir, edited by Begali Qasimaw and Sadir Erkinaw, and Janibek Suwanqulaw and Tahir Qahhar. Tashkent: Ghafur Ghulam namidagi Adabiyat wa San`at Nashriyati, 1996, pp. 39-75, 5,000 copies; also, **San'at (Tashkent) no. 4 (1991). (NN)

36. "Daqlad," Ozbek til wä imla qoroltayining chiqarghan qararlari. Tashkent: Turkistan Jomhoriyäning Däwlät Näshriyati (Eski Shahar Musulman Basmakhanasi), 1922, pp. 35-43. (NNC and NN)

37. "Dar gird-i alifbo-yi nav," Rahbar-i donish no. 10 (1928), pp. 8-10. In Tajik. (DLC and NN)

38. "Dar gird-i alifbo-yi toza," Rahbar-i donish no. 4/5 (1928), pp. 13-16. In Tajik. (DLC and NN)

39. Davra-i hukmroni-yi amir olimkhon. Tashkent-Stalin-abad: Nashriyat-i Davlatii Tajikistan, 1930, in Tajik. Reissued in a new edition prepared by A. Muhiddinov, Dushanbe: Palata-i Davlatii Kitobho 1991, 63 pp., 50,000 copies. Issued also in an Uzbek translation made from the first Tajik version, published in 1930, by H. Qudratilla as Ämir alimkhanning hukmranlik däwri. The recent Uzbek-language reprint came out in Tashkent: Ozbekistan Yazuwchilär Uyushmäsi "Minhaj" Khäyriyä Näshriyati, 1992, 60 pp., 60,000 copies. (NN, reprint only)

Den' strashnogo suda. (See Qiyomat)

40. (U1) "Eng eski (qadimgi) moghul tili lughati." Prepared for the press, but unpublished, evidently.

41. Eng eski turk ädäbiyati nämunäläri. Ädäbiyatimizning tä'rikhi ochon materiyallar. Samarkand: Ozbekistan Däwlät Näshriyatining Näshri; Tashkent: Ozbekistan Mätbä`ä Ishläri Tristining Birinchi Mätbä`äsi, 1927, 124 + IV pp., 5,000 copies. (DLC and NN)

42. (U1) "Ertaklar wa haqiqatlar (Firdawsiyning 1,000 yilligi)," Mash`ala (Tashkent) 1934.

43. (U1) "Eski mäktäblärni nimä qilish keräk?" Qizil ozbekistan (March 6, 1927).

44. (U2) "Färhad wä shirin dastani toghrisidä," Älängä nos. 1/2 (1930).

45. (U1) "Fars ädäbiyatining tärikhi." 1935. Prepared for press, but evidently unpublished.

46. (U2) "Fars ädäbiyati zänjirläri," Ortä asiya ädäbiyati (June 7, 1934). Perhaps a translation of this work: (U1) "Tsep' persidskoi literatury zamknuta," Literatura srednei Azii (1934). In Russian, or, a translated title only.

47. Fars sha`iri `umär khäyyam. [at top of title page:] "Qizil Qalam" Ozbekistan Inqilab Yazuchilar Jäm`iyati." Samarkand-Tashkent: Oz Näshri, 1929, vol. 2, 86 pp., 2,000 copies. (NN)

48. (U2) "Faryod," Bukhoro-yi sharif (June 29 and July 3, 1912). In Tajik.

49. (U2) "Firdawsi," Baro-yi adabiyot-i sotsialisti (Sotsialisticheskaia nauka i tekhnika) nos. 5/6 (1934). In Tajik. Reissued in an edition prepared by Gulmurod Paywandi under the title: Shurish-i vose`. Firdawsiy. Dushanbe: MT.TGU, 1992, 62 pp., 15,000 copies. "Firdawsiy" appears on pp. 40-60 of the pamphlet. (NN, reprint only)

50. (U1) "Firdawsining hayati wa ijadi." Prepared for press but evidently unpublished.

51. (U2) "Firdawsi. Zamon wa muhiti u Baro-yi adabiyot-i sotsialisti (Tashkent) nos. 5/6 (1934). In Tajik.

52. ["Gozälim, bewäfa gulistanim,... (Fatimäjangä) (first line)]. Printed in Ozbekistan ädäbiyati wä sän`äti (Dec. 11, 1987), p. 3; also, Naim Karimaw, Erik Karimaw, and Sherali Turdiew, compilers, Chin sewish (1996), p. 38, place this untitled poem immediately following Mr. Fitrat's contributions to Ozbek yash shairlari (1922) reprinted in their volume. They

do not cite a date or source for "Gozälim...," but it did not appear in Ozbek yash shairlari. (NN, reprint only)

53. (U2) "ʿHälimä' operäsi häqidä," Istirakiyun (Nov. 29, 1920).

54. "Hayot wa ghaye-ye hayot," Ayinä no. 8 (Dec. 14, 1913), pp. 196-97; ibid., no. 9 (Dec. 21, 1913), pp. 220-22. In Tajik. (NN) (U2) Also, Sado-i Sharq (Dushanbe) no. 6 (1989). In Tajik. (NN)

55. "Himmät wä säbati bolmagan millätning häqq-i hayati yoqdur," Ayinä no. 7 (Jan. 14, 1915), pp. 162-165. (NN)

56. Hind ikhtilalchilari. Besh pärdälik fajʿiäli tiyatro. Berlin: Mohärrir-o Nash'ri Bokharali ʿÄbdorrä'of "Fiträt," composed 1920, published 1923., 90 pp. in modified Arabic script. A second edition, prepared by Veli Kajum-Khan and Anna von Gabain as publishers appeared in Grafenhainichen, Germany: R. Herrose's Verlag, 1944, 79 pp. in Roman script. Also, text prepared by Sheräli Turdiyew and republished in Shärq yulduzi no. 4 (1990), pp. 35-59, in the Uzbek Cyrillic alphabet. Another edition appeared in Chin sewish (1996), pp. 76-124. (NN)

Hindistanda... (see Munazirä....)

57. "ʿIbätul-khaqayiq," Mäʿarif wä oqutghuchi no. 10 (1928), pp. 41-46. (DLC and NN)

58. (U2 and T1) "Ikki royhat," Hurriyät no. 35 (Sept. 1, 1917).

59. "Imla känfırensiyäsi munasäbäti bilän," Mäʿarif wä oqutghuchi no. 3 (1928), pp 6-7. (DLC and NN)

60. (U2) "Insaniyät häqidä näwaiy qanday fikrdä," (Tashkent) 1919. (T1) Reprinted in Sirli aläm No. 2 (1991).

61. (T1) "Ingliz oyunlari," Hurriyät no. 64 (?? 1918).

62. (T1) "Ingliz wa turkistan," Hurriyät no. 82 (Mar. 29, 1918).

63. (T1) "Inqilab," Hurriyät no. 54 (Dec. ? 1917).

64. "Iqdomot-e isloh-korone-ye hukumat-e bukhoro," Ayinä no. 8 (Jan. 30, 1915), pp. 198-200. In Tajik. (NN)

65. (T1) "Ish zamani otmasing," Hurriyät no. 52 (Nov. 7, 1917).

66. "Ishqimning ta`rikhi," Ozbek yash sha`irlari... (1922), pp. 10-11. (Lunds Universitetsbibliotek and NN)

67. (U2) "Islahat wä bukhara," Hurriyät (1917).

68. Issledovanie o staroi tiurkskoi literature. Samarkand: 1930. [If this work did not appear separately in Russian as shown, it may have been a translation of Eng eski Turk adabiyati namunalari... (1927), listed above, or, the entry may be a defective reference to the Uzbek version from the Russian-language Bol'shaia sovetskaia entsiklopediia, first edition, vol. 57 (1936), p. 656. Until a copy can be examined, the present Bibliography includes this title as a separate publication in Russian.]

69. (U2) "Istekbol," Bukhoro-yi sharif (July 17, August 14, 1912). In Tajik.

70. (U2 and T1) "Ittifaq etäylik," Hurriyät (Samarkand) no. 46 (July 25, 1917), p. 2. See also Yashlik no. 10 (1990).

71. (U2) "Jähalätgä tä`sibgä," Shora (Orenburg) no. 2 (1917).
In Tatar. (T1) Reprinted in Khälq sozi (Tashkent) Nov. 1991).

72. (U2 and T1) "Jäma`ät wä khäyriyä," [in T1: Jama`at-i
khayriya"] Hurriyät no.72 (Feb. 19, 1918).

73. (U1) Kamal shamsi. Ilmiy handasa. Trans. Abdalrauf
Fitrat. Tashkent: 1920.

74. (with B. S. Sergeev), Kaziiskie dokumenty XVI veka.
Tekst perevod, ukazatel' vstrechaiushchikhsia iuridicheskikh
terminov i primechaniia. Tashkent: Izdatel'stvo Komiteta Nauk
UzSSR, 1937, 80 pp. In Tajik and Russian. (NNC and NN)

75. "Kim deyäi seni?" Ozbek yash sha`irlari..., p. 4. Reprinted
in Turkistan (????OcakJan. 12, 1924). Also in Ozbekistan
ädäbiyati wä sän`äti (Dec. 11, 1987), p. 3. (Lunds Universitets-
bibliotek and NN)

76. (U2) "Kominterngä yash bukharaliklärning III s'ezdidän
telegrämmä" (archive document).

77. Khalq mä`arifi toghrisida lininning oäsiyätläri. `Abdalrauf
Fitrat's translation into Uzbek of N. K. Krupskaia's pamphlet.
Moscow: S.S.S.R. Khälqlärining Märkäz Näshriyati, 1925, 54
pp. (NN)

78. Lenin häm shärq. A translation into Uzbek by `Abdalrauf
Fitrat of Nariman Narimanov's pamphlet. Moscow: SSSR
Khälqlärining Märkäz Näshriyati, 1924, 20 pp. (NN)

79. "Loyaha-yi alifboya naw-i tojiki," Rahbar-i donish no. 3
(Nov. 1927), pp. 12-14. In Tajik. (DLC and NN)

80. (T1) "Ma`arif," Hurriyät no. 56 (Dec. ? 1917).

81. (U2) Mahmud Qashghariy. Dewan-u lughatit turk. Evidently unpublished.

82. (T1) "Mäktäb keräk," Hurriyät no. 86 (April ? 1918).

83. (U2) "Maktub ba idora," Bukhoro-yi sharif (Bukhara) (Apr. 19, 1912). In Tajik.

84. "Manfa`at (Manfi`at)," Ayinä no. 4 (Nov. 17, 1913), pp. 99-100; ibid., no. 6 (Nov. 30, 1913), pp. 149-50. (NN)

85. (U2) "Mäarif ishläri," Uchqun (Eski Bukhara) no. 2 (1923).

86. "Mashrab," Ilmiy fikr no. 1 (May-June 1930), pp 40-57. (DLC and NN)

87. (U2) Mawlud-i sharif, yakhud muroot-i khayrul bajar. Tashkent: 1914. In Tajik.

88. (U2) "Mening kecham," Inqilab (Tashkent) no. 13 (1924).

89. (U1) "Mening tunim," Inqilab nos. 13/14 (1924).

90. *Ming bir kecha. Tanlangan ertaklar. Evidently unpublished.

91. "Me`raj," Khudasizlar no. 1 (1928).

92. "Mirrikh yulduzigä," Ozbek yash sha`irlari... (1922), pp. 7-8. (T1) Reprinted in Ishtirakiyun (1922); also in Ozbekistan ädäbiyati wä sän`äti (Dec. 11, 1987), p. 3. (Lunds Universitetsbibliotek and NN)

93. Moselmanan-e dar al-rahat. trans. by `Abdalrauf Fitrat into Tajik from Esmail Bey Ghasparanski's (Ismail-Bey Gasprinski's) Crimean Tatar novelette written 1891, published 1894, as a supplement to Tarjuman, which appeared in the Tajik

version as "Darur rahat." Petrograd: Ketabkhane-ye Ma`arifat, 1915, 87 pp.

94. "Muhämmäd salih," Älängä no. 10 (1929), pp. 9-12. (DLC and NN)

95. (T1) "Mukhtariyät," Hurriyät no. 57 (Dec. ? 1917).

96. Mukhtasar-i ta'rikh-i Islam. [registered in Knizhnaia letopis' under the main title: Tarikh-Islam] Samarkand: Shukrullah-oghli; Matba`a Gazarof, 1915, 36 pp., 1,100 copies, in Tajik. Reissued in a new edition prepared by Abdulhayi Saidzoda-i Muhammadamin, under the editorship of Academician Muhammadjon Shukuraw. Dushanbe: "Irfon" 1991, 38 pp., 10,000 copies. Also, scholars issued the work in Uzbek translation under the title Mukhtäsär Islam tärikhi. Tashkent: "Nur," 1992, 30 pp., 20,000 copies. (T1) Reprinted in Uzbek translation in 1928. (NN, reprints only)

Munazira... (see Munozira....)

97. Munozira. Muddaris-e bukhoro-ye bo yak nafar-e farangi dar hindiston dar bora'ye maktab-e jadidä. Istanbul: Matb`ä'-e Islamiyä'-e Hikmat, H.1327 [A.D. 1911-12]., 64 + 4 pp. Published in Russian translation by Col. Iagello under the title Spor bukharskago mudarrisa s evropeitsem v Indii o novome-todnykh shkolakh. Istinnyi rezultat obmena myslei. Trans. to Russian by Col. Iagello. Tashkent: Elektro-Parovaia Tipogra-fiia-Litografiia, Shtabs Okruga, 1911, 98 pp. Also, translated and abridged from Tajik to Turki by Mu`allim Hajji Mu`in ibn-i Shukrullah Samarqandi under the title Hindistandä bir färängi

ilä bukharali bir muddärisning bir nichä mäs'älälär häm usul-i jädidä khususidä qilgan munazäräsi, and published in Tashkent: Izdatel'stvo Knizhnoi Torgovli Turkestana. Litografiia V. M. Il'ina, H1331/A.D.1914, 41 pp., 2,200 copies. Reissued in an edition prepared by Gulmurod Payvandi under the title Munozara. Haqiqat natija-i tasodum-i afkor ast. Dushanbe: TGU, 1992, 55 pp. In Tajik. Also, reissued in Uzbek under the title: "Hindistandä bir färängi ilä bukharali mudärrisning jädid mäktäbläri khususindä qilgan munazaräsi," in Shärq yulduzi no. 1 (1997), pp. 117-165. (NNC and NN)

"Muqaddas qan." (See "Qan.")

98. "Muqaddimat-ul adab," Ma`arif wä oqutghuchi nos. 7/8 [T1: no. 10] (1926). (DLC and NN)

99. (U2 and T1) "Musulmanlär, ghafil qalmäng," Hurriyät no. 33 (Aug. 25, 1917). See also Yashlik No. 10 (1991).

100. Nähw. Ozbek tili qa'idalari toghrisida bir täjribä. Ikinchi kitäb. Samarkand-Tashkent: Ozbekistän Däwlät Näshriyäti, 1st ed., 1925; 2d ed., 1926, 52 pp., 5,000 copies; ibid., 3d printing, 1927, 55 pp., 7,000 copies. ** ibid., Tashkent-Samarkand: 1930. (DLC and NN)

Narimanov (see Lenin....)

101. "Nawayining fars sha`irlighi häm uning fars diwani toghrisida," Mä`arif wa oqutghuchi no. 12 (1926). (DLC and NN)

102. "Negä boylä?" Ozbek yash sha`irlari... (1922), pp. 13-14. Reprinted in Ozbekistan ädäbiyati wä sän`äti (Dec. 11, 1987), p. 3. (Lunds Universitetsbibliotek and NN)

103. Oghuzkhan. 1919. Termed an opera, perhaps because music accompanied it. Actors presented a scene from it in connection with a festival of old plays put on in March 1935 by the Hamza Academic Theater on what it termed its "Fifteenth Anniversary." Evidently unpublished, **except for a fragment that appeared in Yash leninchi (Tashkent) (March 10, 1935).

104. "Ogut," Ozbek yash sha`irlari..., (1922), p. 23. (U2) reports a reprint of it also in Elbek's Gozäl yazghichlär (därslik). Tashkent: 1925 (sic). Reprinted in Chin sewish (1996), p. 36. (Lunds Universitetsbibliotek and NN)

105. "XVI-nchi [On altinchi] äsrdän songghä ozbek ädäbiyatigä umumiy bir qäräsh," Älängä nos. 8/9 (1929), pp. 6-8. (DLC and NN)

106. "Oqutghuchilar yurtigha," Ozbek yash sha`irlari... (1922), p. 24. (Lunds Universitetsbibliotek and NN)

107. (U2) Oquw. Ibtidaiy oquw maktablarining songgi sinflari uchun. Baku: 1917. In Turki (later, Uzbek). (Dudoignon, 1996, p. 205) cites, with confusing transliteration, a rather similar title issued in Central Asia that year: Uqu! Ibtida`i maktablaring sung ichun yazildi. Bukhara: Ma`rifat Kitabkhanasi, 1917. Presumably, the same schoolbook printed in two cities.

108. (U1) "Orta Asiyada yer munasabati tarikhidan materiyallar." Prepared for press, but evidently unpublished.

109. (U1) "Orta Asiyaning sugharilish tarikhidan uch hujjat (unfinished and unannounced). But, see below his Russian-language Tri dokumenta po agrarnomu voprosu...

110. Ozbek ädäbiyati nämunäläri. Samarkand-Tashkent: Oznäshr, 1928, vol. I, 319 pp., 5,000 copies. (Istanbul Univ., Edebiyat Fakültesi Kütüphanesi and NN)

111. (U1) "Ozbek adabiyati tarikhi (feadalizm dawri)." 1934. Prepared for press, but evidently unpublished.

112. Ozbek ädäbiyatigä `a'id qira'ät kitabi. n.p.: Däwlät `Ilmiy Shorasi, I bolim; II bolim (1928).

113. Ozbek qilassiq muwsiqasi wä uning tä'rikhi. Samarkand-Tashkent: Ozbekistan Däwlät Näshriyati, 1927, 80 pp., 3,053 copies, illustrated. At top of title page: Ozbekstan `Ilmiy Märkäzining Ozbeklärni Orgänish Qomitasi Tä'rikh Änjumäni. A new edition prepared under the auspices of the Ozbeklär Orgänish Qomitäsi reprinted the 1927 edition without change except to use the Uzbek modified Cyrillic alphabet in place of the modified Arabic of the first edition. Tashkent: Ozbekistan Respublikäsi Fänlär Akädemiyäsi "Fän" Näshriyati, 1993, 56 pp., 3,000 copies. (DLC and NN)

114. "Ozbek musiqasi toghrisida," Älängä no. 2 (Feb. 1928), p. 14. (DLC and NN)

115. (U2) "Ozbek sha`iri turdiy," Mä`arif wä oqutghuchi no. 12 (1928).

116. (U2) "Ozbekchä til säbaqligi," Qizil ozbekistan (Apr. 30, 1926).

117. (U1 and U2) "Ozbek tilining särfi toghrisidä," Qizil ozbekistan (July 9, 1925). Announced but perhaps unpublished.

118. Ozbek yash sha`irlari. (Shi`rlar toplami). Tashkent: Turkistan Däwlät Näshriyati, 1922, pp. 3-24. These poems received republication in part or in full in Erklik yulduzi. She'rlär. Tashkent: Ghafur Ghulam namidagi Adabiyat wa San'at Nashriyati, 1994, pp. 25-30; Abdurauf Fitrat, Chin sewish. She`rlär, drämälär, mäqalalär, edited by Begäli Qasimaw and Sadir Erkinaw, Janibek Suwanqulaw and Tahir Qähhar. Tashkent: Ghäfur Ghulam namidägi Adäbiyat wä Sän`ät Näshriyati, 1996, pp. 23-37. (Lunds Universitetsbibliotek and NN)

119. (U2) "Pakhta," Orta asiya adabiyati (Tashkent) (Nov. 21, 1933); and in Ozbekistan adabiyati. (Tashkent), part 1, 1934.

120. "Parcha," Ozbek yash sha`irlari... (1922), p. 17. (Lunds Universitetsbibliotek and NN)

121. (U2) Qädimgi turk ädäbiyati izlänishläri. Samarkand: 1930.

122. Qan (Muqäddäs qan). 1917. Various sources give the date of its composition as 1915, 1917, 1920 or 1921. Evidently, no one ever published the play, though contemporaries knew it well, but research has not uncovered a copy of the full work.

123. "Qar," Uchqun. She'rlar toplami. Moscow: n.p., 1921.

(U2) "Qar," Uchqun no. 2 (1923). Also reprinted in a school textbook prepared by Elbek, Gozäl yazghichlär (därslik). Tashkent: 1924.

124. (T1) "Qarä khäbär," no. 43 Hurriyät (1917). Qashghariy (see Mahmud; see "Qotadgho...")

125. Qiyamät (khäyali hikayä). Preface by Därwish (i.e., Nadhir Toraqol-uli). Moscow: Millät Ishläri Kämisärligi qashida "Märkäziy Shärq Näshriyati," 1923, 28 pp., 5,000 copies. Second Uzbek edition, entitled Qyamat. Hayaly hkaya. Tashkent: OzSSR Dawlat Nashriyati, 1935, 32 pp., 50,125 copies, illustrated. This seems to be the first known reissue, but with numerous alterations, of the 2d Uzbek version (1935). Or, it could be a new translation from the 1936 Tajik version. The present version appeared in the blatantly anti-religious collection of selections from Hamza Hakim Zada Niyaziy, Abdulla Qadiriy, Ghafur Ghulam, Kamal Yashin, Zulfiya, and others: Yengämiz khurafatni bid'ätni, compiled by Wähab Rozimäta. Tashkent OzSSR Däwlät Bädiiy Adäbiyat Näshriyati, 1961, pp. 29-47. An Uzbek-language Qiyamat was reissued in Tashkent, 1972 and also probably later. (NN)

126. (U2) "Qiyshiq eshan," Khudasizlar nos. 2-3 (1930).

127. Qiyomat. [added on back title page:] Antireligioznye rasskazy. Stalinabad-Leningrad: Nashriyyoti Davlatiyi Tojikis-ton, 1936, 38 pp., 5,000 copies, illustrated. In Tajik. Reissued in Dushanbe: Tadzhikgosizdat, 1964, 31 pp., 15,000 copies, and again in Dushanbe: "Irfon," 1969, 34 pp., 8,000 copies.

Repeated editions in Russian translation, including Strashnyi sud (satiristicheskii rasskaz). Trans. L. Kandinov. Dushanbe: "Irfon," 1964, 47 pp. 15,000 copies; and, Den' strashnogo suda. Rasskaz-satira. Moscow: Politizdat, 1965, 32 pp. 260,000 copies. (NNC and NN)

128. (U2) "Qiz qatili," written 1932, evidently unpublished. ** A similar title, "Qizlär qatili. Hikayä," appeared in Ortä asiya khälqlär ädäbiyati nos. 2-4 (1933).

129. (U2 and T1) "Qizil tilli qazimizning hakimanä nutqläri munasäbäti bilän," Hurriyät no. 30 (Aug. 15, 1917).

130. "Qotadgho bilik," Mä`arif wä oqutghuchi no. 2 (1925), pp. 68-74. (DLC and NN)

131. Qoyidaho-yi zabon-i tojik (sarf wa nahw). Tashkent: 1930. In Tajik. (Helisinki University Library).

132. "Qur'an," Ayinä no. 16 (June 15, 1915), pp. 443-445. (NN)

133. Rähbär-i näjat. Petrograd: Munzim Bukhariy; M. N. Makhsutaw Basmakhanasi, 1915, 224 pp. In Tajik. Reissued in abridged translation to Uzbek prepared and edited by Docent Näzrullä Yoldashew: Bukhara: Bukhara Näshriyati, 1996, 77 pp., 400 copies, illustrated. (NN, reprint only)

134. Rozälär. Samarkand-Tashkent: Oznäshr, 1930.

135. "Sän`ätning mänshä'i (kelib chiqishi)," Mä`arif wä oqutghuchi no. 5 (1927), pp. 37-40. (DLC and NN)

136. Särf. Ozbek tili qa`idalari toghrisida bir täjribä. [On title page:] Ozbekistan Jumhuriyätining Mä`arif Qomisarlighi

khuzuridägi Bilim Ozägi tamanidan mäktäblärdä oqumaq uchun mooafiq korildi. Samarkand-Tashkent: Ozbekistan Däwlät Näshriyati, 1926, book 1, 4th printing, 59 pp., 6,000 copies. Other editions include: ibid., 1925; ibid., Samarkand-Tashkent: Ozbekistan Däwlät Näshriyati, 1927, 5th ed., Book 1, ii and 62 pp., 10,000 copies. (DLC and NN)

137. (U1) Sarf-i zabon-i tajiki. Samarkand, 1925. In Tajik.

138. "Sargudhasht-i tojik-i kambaghal yoke odine," ["Sarsukhan"] Sargudhasht-i yak tojik-i kambaghal yoke odine, [Fitrat's introduction to Sadriddin 'Ayniy's novel, issued again in 1931. Fayzullah Khoja's introduction replaced Fitrat's in the 1930 Russian-language translation.] Samarkand-Dushanbe: Nashriyyot-i Davlati-yi Tojikiston, 1927, 141 pp. 3,000 copies. ibid., 1931. (DLC and NN)

139. (U2) "Sayfi isfarangi," Rahbar-i donish no. 3 (1928). In Tajik.

140. (B1) Säyhä. Istanbul: n.p. 1329/1911, 16 pp. In Tajik. Said to be Fitrat's second publication, after Munazira (1910), above.

141. (U1) "Säyhä. She'rlar turkumi," Säda-i turkistan (July 1914).

142. "Säylaw yäqinläshdi," Hurriyät no. 29 (Aug. 11, 1917), (T1) no. 32 (Aug. 23, 1917). See also Häyat wä iqtisad No. 1 (1990). Cyrillic text of Aug. 11th segment prepared by Dr. Sheräli Turdiyew and reprinted in Hurriyät (Feb. 12, 1997), p. 3. (NN, reprint only)

143. "Shaʿir," Ozbek yash shaʿirlari... (1922), pp. 15-16. Reprinted in Ozbekistan ädäbiyati wä sänʿäti (Dec. 11, 1987), p. 3. (Lunds Universitetsbibliotek and NN)

144. "Sharq," Ozbek yash shaʿirlari... (1922), pp. 19-21. Reissued in Ozbekistan ädäbiyati wä sänʿäti (Dec. 11, 1987), p. 3. (Lunds Universitetsbibliotek and NN)

145. Shärq siyasäti. Calligraphy by ʿAbdalqadi Murad. n.p. [Tashkent:] Tarqatghuchi: Yash Bukharalilar Qomitasining Nashriyat Shuʿbäsi, 1919, 47 pp. (CaQMM and NN)

146. (U1) "Shärq siyasäti," Ishtirakiyun (Oct. 25, 26, 1919; Jan. 29, 1920).

147. "Shärqdä shahmät," Älängä nos. 3/4 (1928), pp. 16-17. (T1) Reprinted in Shärq yulduzi no. 2 (1990). (DLC and NN)

148. "Shash maqam," Maʿarif wä oqutghuchi no. 2 (1925), pp. 94-95. (DLC and NN)

149. Shäytanning tängrigä ʿisyani. Tashkent: Orta Asiya Däwlät Näshriyati, 1924, 20 pp., 5,000 copies. (NNC and NN)

150. (U2) "Sheʿr," Qutulish. Tashkent: 1920.

151. U1 and U2 "Sheʿr wa shaʿirlik. Adabiy musahaba," Ishtirakiyun (July 24, 25, Aug. 30, 1919).

152. (U2 and T1) "Shora-yi islamiyäning khätasi," Hurriyät no. 36 (Sept. 5, 1917).

153. Shurish-i voseʿ [Is'yan-i voseʿ]. Chor pärdä. Yak fojʿiaʿyi tarikhi az hayot-i tajikho-yi ki dar zer farmon-i amiron-i bukhoro budand. In pyisaʿyi awwalin-i tojik. Peshkash-i besharif sol dahum jashn inqilab-i oktabr. Samarkand-

Dushanbe: Nashriyat-i Dawlatii Tojikiston, 1927, 2070 copies. In Tajik. Reissued in a new edition, prepared by Gulmurod Paywandi, under the title Shurish-i vose`. Dushanbe: MT. TGU, 1992, 62 pp., 15,000 copies. (NN)

154. (U1) "Siyasiy hallar," Hurriyät (Samarkand) no. 49 (Nov. 7, 1917).

155. (U1) "Sabiq Bukhara khanligidä yer munasäbäti mäteriyälläri (not announced)

Spor... (see Munazirä...)

Strashnyi sud. (See Qiyomat)

156. (T1) "Sulh uchun," Hurriyät no. 45 (Sept. 29, 1917).

157. (U2) "Täktikä. Yash bukharaliklärning III s'ezdi qärari" (archive dokument).

158. (U2) "Ta`rikh-i adabiyot-i eron," Rahbar-i donish no. 3 (1928).

159. "Taziyane-ye ta'dib," Ayinä no. 13 (Jan. 18, 1914), pp. 214-216. In Tajik. (NN)

160. (T1) "Tädrijgä qärshi," Tang no. 2 (1920).

161. (U2) "Telegramma V. I. Leninu ot III s'ezda mlado-bukhartsev-kommunistov (bol'shevikov). (museum document copy)

162. "Temur aldinda," Hurriyät no. 47 (1917).

163. (U2) Temurning saghanasi(gha). Bir pardali drama/opera. Tashkent: n.p., 1918/1919. Evidently unpublished and lost, except for a fragment printed in Yash leninchi (March 10, 1935).

164. "Tilimiz," Ishtirakiyun no. 32 (June 12, July 12, Aug. 23, 1919). Part 1 reproduced by Hämidulla Baltäbayew in Ozbekistan ädäbiyati wä sän'äti (May 4, 1990), p. 5. The June 12th portion also reprinted in Chin sewish (1996), pp. 237-41. (NN, reprints only)

165. (U1) Tolqin. Opera librettosi. 1934 [1936?]. Perhaps published but lost. Sewärä Käramätilläkhojäewä, in "Qälbimgä mängu muhrlängän... Äbduräuf Fiträt häqidä khatirälär," Täfäkkur no. 2 (1996), p. 69, writes that "in the second half of the 1930s [my father, Abdurauf Fitrat]..., worked in artistic partnership with the composer Mukhtar Äshräfiy in order to create an opera concerning the history of the Bukharan Amirate. It was called 'The Wave' ('Tolqin'), and he wrote the opera libretto for it. Its premiere was held, and an honorarium was received for the libretto. But the work did not see the stage again – they took my father to prison. Shortly after this, the opera received criticism. In it it was regretted with apologies that 'a work by an enemy of the people was put on stage' [and] many times it was complained that financial means had been squandered [on it]. After years passed, I asked Mukhtar Äshräfiy about the fate of the opera libretto. Äshräfiy answered, saying: 'I burned it up at once, right then'!"

166. "Tri dokumenta po agrarnomu voprosu v Srednei Azii," [Leningrad:] Zapiski Instituta Vostokovedeniia Akademii Nauk SSSR book 2 (1933), pp. 69-87. Documents in Tajik, text and translations in Russian. (DLC and NN)

"Tsep' persidskoi literatury zamknuta." (See Fars adabiyati zanjirlari, above.)

167. (T1) "Turk musiqasi toghrisida," Älängä no. 2 (1928).

168. (U1) "Turkistan mukhtariyäti," Hurriyät no. 57 [no. 58 in T1] (Dec. 8, 1917).

169. (T1) "Turkistanda ruslar," Hurriyät nos. 63-54 (Jan. ? 1918)

170. (U2) "Uchinchi s`ezdning bir qärari munasäbäti bilän," Hurriyät no. 28 (Aug. 4, 1917).

171. (U1) Uchqun. She`rlar toplami. Moscow: 1921. (T1) in Turkish of Turkiye.

172. (T1) "Taqsim-i amal," Hurriyät no. 67 (? ? 1918)

173. "Tuzguchidän bir ikki soz," Ozbek ädäbiyati nämunäläri. Samarkand-Tashkent: Oznäshr, 1928, vol. 1, pp. XI-XIII. (Istanbul University, Edebiyat Fakültesi library and NN)

174. Ulughbeg. Piyassa. Post-1917. Attacked by Rahmat Majidi in the volume Literaturnyi Uzbekistan no. 1 (1936), p. 173.

175. "Umär Khäyyam," Qzil Qalam majmu`äsi Samarkand: Oznäshr, 1928, vol. 1.

176. ["U nas dzhigitstvo,"] Tang (Zhurnal TsK Bukharskoi Kompartii), no. 2 (1920). In Turki.

177. "Yänä yandim....," Ozbek yash sha`irlari... (1922), pp. 11-12. (Lunds Universitetsbibliotek and NN)

178. (T1) "Yängi hukumät," Hurriyät no. 52 (Dec. ? 1917).

179. "Yapishmägän gäjäklär. J. Baybolätawgä achiq khät," Qzil Ozbekistan nos. 215-216 (Sept. 15-16, 1929). A part reprinted in Yashlik no. 5 (1990), in XX äsr ozbek ädäbiyati (mäjmuä), compiled by N. Kärimaw, B. Näzaräw, T. Niyazmetawä and U. Narmätaw (Tashkent: "Oqituwchi," 1993), pp. 48-53; and, in Chin sewish (1996), pp. 242-52. (NN, reprints only)

180. "Yäsäwi mäktäbi sha`irlari toghrisida tekshirishlär," Mä`arif wä oqutghuchi nos. 5/6 (1928), pp. 49-52. (DLC and NN) 181. (U2) "Yash bukharaliklärning II s'ezdi qärari" (archive document).

182. (U2) "Yash bukharaliklärning III s'ezdi" (archive document).

183. (T1) "Yashirin muahädälär," Hurriyät no. 55 (Dec. ? 1917).

184. (T1) "Yashlar wazifa bashlang!" Hurriyät no. 27 (1917).

185. "Yighla Islam." Tashkent: n.p., 1919. (T1) published in Ishtirakiyun 1919/1920?

186. "Yek takhattur-i alim," 1920, reproduced in Sadriddin `Ayniy, Namuna-i adabiyyat-i Tajik. Moscow: Chapkhana-i Nashriyyat-i Markaz-i Khalq, 1926, p. 581.

187. "Yurt qayghusi (bir ozbek yigitining tilindän)," Hurriyät (Samarkand) (July 28, 1917); ibid., (Aug. 18, 1917), p. 2; ibid., (Oct. 31, 1917). (T1) Republished in Hurriyät no. 2 (1918); also in Fän wä turmush no. 7 (1990); also in Turan tärikhi. Ammäbap majmua (July 20, 1992), p. 7; and, also the part

published in August 1917, in Erklik yulduzi. She'rlär, edited by Tahir Qähhar. Tashkent: Ghäfur Ghulam namidägi Adäbiyat wä Sän'ät Näshriyati, 1994, pp. 22-24. (NN, reprint only)

188. (U1) "Za chutkuiu literaturnuiu sredu," Literatura srednei Azii, 1933. In Russian.

189. "Zähraning imani," Khudasizlar no. 2 (1928). A new edition prepared by Näim Kärimaw was printed in Fän wä turmush no. 7 (1988), pp. 10-11.

190. (U2) "`Zahhak-i märan' munasäbäti ilä," Ishtirakiyun (Oct. 23, 1919).

191. "Zäid wä zäynäb," Khudasizlar no. 4 (1928), pp. 28-33; ibid., no. 5 (1928). (DLC and NN)

« تورک یوردی » اداره‌سینه هدیه در .

هندستانده بر فرنگی ایله بخارالی بر مدرسنک

بر نیچه مسئله لر هم اصول جدیده ختنه‌صیده قیلغان

مناظره

سی

محرری: فطرت

مترجمی: معلم حاجی معين ابن شكر الله سمرقندی

ناشری: ترکستان کتبخانه‌سی

بونچی طبع

تکرار طبعی مترجم شرکتیله ناشرلریکه مخصوص در

۱۳۳۱ هجری
۱۳۱۲ ملادیه

ТАШКЕНТЪ.

Типо-Литографія В. М. Ильинъ.

1913 г.

Figure 1. Title page of 1913 Turki translation, from the Tajik/Persian of
`Abdalraufs <u>Dispute</u> (*Munazara*) (1910), by Hajji Mu`in ibn-i
Shukrullah Samarqandi (this title page autographed by Hajji Mu`in, the
translator, a very prominent Reformist of the Period)

Figure 2. 1,000 (ming)-som Banknote (1922) of the Bukhara People's Conciliar Republic, bearing the official signature of Treasury Minister Fitrat.

Абд-ур-Рауфъ.

РАЗСКАЗЫ

ИНДІЙСКАГО ПУТЕШЕСТВЕННИКА

(Бухара, какъ она есть).

Переводъ съ персидскаго А. Н. КОНДРАТЬЕВА.

Изданіе Махмудъ-Ходжа Бегбуди.

Самаркандъ.
Типо-лит. Т-ва Б. Газаровъ и К. Соловов.
1913.

Figure 3. Contemporary Russian Edition – issued in Samarkand by Reformist
leader, Mahmud Khoja Behbudiy in 1913 – of `Abdalrauf Fitrat's Tales
of a Hindustan Traveler (*Boyonat-i sayyoh-i hindi*), first published in
Tajik/Persian, Istanbul, 1911/12

ئۇزبېكستان دەۋلەت عىلمى كېڭەشى

ئوزبېك ئەدەبىياتى نەمۇنەلەرى

I ىنچى جىلد

ئۆزگەنى: فىترەت

ئۆزنەشر
تاشكەنت 1928 ىل سەمەرقەند

Figure 4. <u>Specimens of Uzbek Literature</u> (*Ozbek ädäbiyati nämunälari*) (1928), compiled by Professor Fitrat, furiosly denounced by communist critics for its lack of a Marxist approach to literary history and analysis